Options Trading:

A Quick and Easy Guide for Beginners to Start Trading

Pete Manlow

Table of Contents

Introduction

Congratulations on buying *Options Trading: A Quick and Easy Guide for Beginners to Start Trading* and thank you for doing so.

The following chapters will discuss the massive world of options trading. You're here because for one reason or another, you wanted to learn about options trading. Maybe you're a finance student looking to get a better grasp on this concept for a class that you're taking or a test that you have coming up. Maybe you're just somebody wanting to get a better idea about what options trading even is so that you're more financially savvy. Maybe you're a person looking for a refresher on all there is to know about options trading so that you can quickly get yourself back up to speed.

Regardless of what your reasoning is, you've come to the right place. I can guarantee you one thing by the end of this book: you're going to have a firm grasp on everything that there is to know about options trading.

Before we get into this, I feel I must warn you: options trading is one of the riskiest forms of trading. There are multiple reasons for this, and these can only really be explained once I've gone more into what options exactly *are* in the first place. However, the key point is that options are most people who trade options will end up losing money, for the simple reason that options play *against* time, where stocks generally benefit from the passage of time.

However, if with the knowledge that options are riskier than stocks, you'd still like to learn about them and how to work with them, then this is most certainly the book for you. We're going to be covering what there is to know about options trading so that you can go from an options trading zero to an options trading hero in no time. And indeed, if your field of study has to do with finance or trading in general, then you'd do very well to learn everything that you can about this highly risky, very tricky form of securities trading.

There are plenty of books on this subject on the market, thanks again for choosing this one! Every effort was made to ensure it is full of as much useful information as possible, please enjoy!

Chapter 1: Basic Explanation and History

Before we get into the modern caveats of options, we need to understand in the simplest terms possible what they are and how they grew to where they are today. This means setting ourselves up with a basic definition.

Options are admittedly tricky. This is for the simple reason that historically, the economy deals with absolutes. When you look at the way that economies have risen up and formulated, it's always been based off of the trading of commodities - commodities being defined as the end result of a form of labor to turn a raw resource into something else. A commodity could be anything from a wooden table, which is the end result of the labor which went into developing that table from the wood and using the screws to put it together, to the wood which defines that table in the first place, which is the end result of the labor of harvesting the raw resource of lumber and wood from forests. In this respect, commodities are what have made up the bulk of the economy.

Money has had quite a long journey itself. Social economies started out from the concept of barter. One thing was traded for another thing and the economy existed within a system of absolutes. I *absolutely* have a bushel of apples, which I am willing to trade another person who *absolutely* has a bucket of goat's milk. In this respect, commodities were traded absolutely without the need for a mediator. Money slowly became introduced into the equation.

The line between commodities traded for a requisite value, as in the barter system, and the first early` money systems can be very blurred. After all, this is all just a method of trading the unwanted for another unwanted. However, the concept of a "coincidence of wants" would pop up, which is essentially the concept that things don't always follow a linear timetable and certain things which would be normally traded for another will often spoil one before the other. This led to the need for an intermediate commodity, and thus the idea of commodity money - money with an intrinsic value representing a given exchange value - was born.

The first conceptions of money were instilled in the usage of early coinage. This actually popped up in Mesopotamia rather early in its history, where a certain amount of gold or similarly precious metal would stand in for a certain amount of grain within a local granary, generally barley. However, more standardized mediums of exchange which would find themselves useful and in demand year round, such as but not limited to copper, gold, silver, and wine. The linguistic impact of these specific means of exchange continues to persist elementally within modern language and culture. Take, for example, the French word *argent*, which can mean both *silver*, in reference to the element and the metal, as well as *money*, as in the phrase "gagner d'argent" meaning "to be paid" or, literally, "to win money".

Over time, money came to be represented through paper. This practice has its roots in China, where the usage of paper to represent arbitrary values of other things such as gold would pop up. This practice would eventually spread. Paper money generally first came to European culture through the Scandinavian countries where ore was abundant and carrying metal with you would actually prove to be very heavy and cumbersome. Instead, exchange notes representing these same quantities were substituted, which began the journey of money as we know it today.

The thing which happened with money represents another ideal entirely which ties very heavily back to the development of *options* trading, and which is a fundamental lesson in what options are and how and why they're used. The development of money represented an essential separation: the separation between the finite and the abstract. The finite barter economy where tangible goods were swapped with and for tangible goods represented an ideal that would end up to have a great many essential problems entangled with it. Among these is the notion of the aforementioned coincidence of wants. In order to develop the concept of year round exchange, it was necessary to form an essential detachment between the tangible good to be exchanged by, as stated, the development of a third variable, a third mediator commodity which replaces the finite qualities of other tradable commodities in favor of infinite qualities such as tradability and a sense of *vague value* - a mutable definition of immutable usefulness, such that in the currency's vague value an infinite set of possible solutions can be derived from its very use.

As a result of this development of vague values and finite tradability of an item with theoretically infinite value came the essential detachment I've been speaking of, the demarcation of where the tangible real use value - the perceived value of a commodity and its usefulness insofar as the person who is buying and selling it perceives it - of a given object is translated into a demonstrable exchange value expressed solely through the usage of currency. This detachment can best be referred to as the transition of comparing two items' subjective use values to the linear development of items receiving objective exchange values through the usage of market mechanisms.

Options trading represents a necessarily similar detachment: options represent a given *exchange* value of an object, and the necessary promise that an object can be bought and sold at that given value at a future date. In other words, it's a binding securities contract that allows you to say ahead of time what value you are willing to buy or sell an object for.

This is important to realize because this central concept of options trading is the historical point at which these two notions of use value and exchange value began to separate entirely. The entire idea of options trading specializes in the separation of the tangible *notion* of a commodity from the intangible *selling* price of a commodity.

I'll say it this way: let's say that you have a bushel of corn. As last reported, a bushel of corn costs approximately $3.65. By next season, this cost could go up, or it could go down. The bushel of corn is still going to represent the same quantity and the same weight of corn in the next season: that amount of that commodity will be the same, and that commodity will still be exactly the same as it is at the time of the contract. However, the given exchange value of the corn will indeed be different, assuming non-vacuum conditions because economics doesn't, and never has, existed within a vacuum. The price will go up, or the price will go down. What exactly happens depends highly upon the market forces which are at work. But, the price will most definitely not be the same.

What an options contract does is it takes this variable aspect - the notion of shifting exchange values - and makes it an absolute. An options contract says that, regardless of the economic "weather", the commodity will sell for a given price on a given date, flat, period, full stop. Note that it's also important to remember that there are also *stock options*, which function *similarly* to commodity options but instead act as a means of

There's a bit more to it: options mean that the buyer or seller of the commodity has the *option*, or the *choice*, to buy or sell the commodity for that value. It doesn't mean, however, the obligation; the buyer or seller is under absolutely no obligation to *actually* purchase or sell the stock at that price, the options contract merely means that the possibility is, in fact, there.

Options have a long history, and are the most prolific of any securities in human history. In fact, there's reason to believe that they're the *first* securities system developed in human history. They have their roots in even early human society.

The first recorded instance of the usage of options was when Greek great Thales of Miletus decided to take advantage of the olive harvest. The story goes that Thales had caught wind of the prediction that the next season would garner a far larger olive harvest than the usual. Prior to the harvest, he sought out the exclusive right to olive presses come harvest time. When the olive harvest came around and the size of it was indeed much bigger than usual, he took advantage of his rights to the olive presses in order to rent the presses out at a higher rate since the demand of use was far greater due to the far larger harvest.

Options have had a nominal use ever since the notion of markets and monetary exchange. Their tens of hundreds of years of usage has built them to be a very usable and successful market instrument in terms of speculating and hedging (we'll talk more about what these mean in just a second). However, they've had quite a bumpy road to get where they are today. The biggest example of options and futures being quite risky is in the Dutch tulip market bubble, largely regarded as one of the first, if not *the* first, major speculative bubble in human history.

Essentially, what happened was that tulips were incredibly valuable in Europe, especially the Netherlands during the time after it had recently established sovereignty from Spain and found itself having a huge amount of trade fortunes known primarily as the *Dutch Golden Age*, wherein the Netherlands found itself being cast as the epicenter of the East Indies trade that dominated Europe; during this time, one voyage alone would often be able to yield profits as high as four-hundred percent.

During this time is actually when tulips actually gained status as a very high-end luxury item.

To understand how this entire process works, you have to understand the cultivation process for tulips. Tulips are generally grown from their bulbs and spread by way of tulip seeds and tulip buds. When a given tulip bud grows up to be a flower, the original tulip bud actually disappears, with a copycat bud, as well as several other buds, and these actually - if properly taken care of and cultivated - will spread to produce new tulips. The process for a seed to grow into a bulb, however, will take about 7 to 12 years, which is quite a long time.

Given the fact that these were the most vivid, colorful, and beautiful flowers in Europe, they began to be highly sought after. The time to grow a tulip on one's own was, of course, far too long, so many opted to instead by the already grown tulips from others, specifically the tulip bulbs which would flower in the dormant period from early summer to early fall.

The flowers would continue to grow and grow in popularity as a result of their high social status. Because of this, professional tulip growers began to pay more and more for certain tulip bulbs with certain coloration patterns that made them even prettier than normal. As time went on, the price of these tulips went up as well, but since the demand for those tulips went up, the price of *normal* tulip bulbs went up as well. After a while, tulip bulbs of any sort were selling for absolutely absurd amounts.

This same year, the notion of a *futures contract* sprang up in the Netherlands. This is basically an options trade; the only differentiating factor is that, while the options trader is *not* obligated to go through and buy or sell for the stated amount, the buyer in the *futures contract* is obligated to buy, and the seller is obligated to sell.

This rudimentary form of speculation in the Netherlands would turn out to be an actual fundamental economic crisis. This was also one of the first modern instances of that detachment that I was talking about: when one bought a futures contract for a tulip bulb, they were only buying the hypothetical concept of a tulip bulb that they would receive later. This entire thing happened without any sort of actual exchange of tulip bulbs. Whether this is bizarre or inspiring to you depends on your own personal leanings on political economy. Regardless of one's personal feelings, though, this entire thing would end up being cataclysmic.

The price of tulip bulbs would end up shooting even *higher* due to the speculation of tulip future contracts. A great many people would both make and lose entire swaths of money overnight. This was the swelling of the bubble; the absurd amounts of speculation which made tulip bulbs extremely expensive for no reason other than the market itself.

The bubble, as all do, would eventually burst. In the late period of 1636 on the eve of 1637, and slipping somewhat into the next year, tulip bulb prices started to hit a relative peak.

However, the contracts made in this period would not actually be carried out, either. This is due to the fact that around February 3rd of 1637, the tulip bulb contract prices would crash completely, causing the exchange of tulip futures contracts to come to a complete stop.

The crash began in the area of Haarlem in north Holland. Here, for the first time ever, buyers wouldn't show up to a given tulips contract auction. There are various reasons given for this, but the most commonly accepted is that there was a chronic pandemic in Haarlem: the bubonic plague. The fact that Haarlem was at the apex of the given outbreak may have been the very reason that the speculative tulips bubble burst.

After the tulip futures contracts bubble, a lot of anti-speculatory rhetoric would persist throughout Europe. In fact, this very economic tragedy - which tanked the economy of Holland, sent it into a recession, and lost entire life savings of commoners - is one of the main reasons that speculatory contracts such as options contracts and futures contracts weren't practiced on a particularly large scale and were even feared for the next three hundred years to follow. However, options trading has come back in the United States as a form of large scale trading. It wasn't so much that it was taken unserious but rather that it was pushed to the wayside in favor of other methods of trade.

The Chicago Board Options Exchange was established in the 1970s, specifically 1970, to facilitate options trading on United States soil by the usage of a set of intensive standards for both forms and terms, as well as by the establishment of a guaranteed clearinghouse through which trade may be conducted.

Because of this establishment, there has been a massive upturn in both commercial and academic interest in the contexts of selling and buying of options contracts. A great many options exchanges have cropped up in America, and the usage of over the counter smaller and less standardized options agreements have also increased by quite a bit.

Chapter 2: Basic Options Theory

So now that we've established how and why options exist, as well as what basic purpose they serve, it's about time that we start to talk about the basics of their structure as well as what a modern *options contract* really means, especially in United States terms where a lot of options trading takes place and where, statistically, you're most likely to be reading this book from.

There are a great many parts to an options contract, in short. Of course, we've already talked about what options are in the most general possible sense, but we haven't quite talked about what the precise usage of these options would be, especially in modern economic terms.

The gist is that options have two major parts: *calls* and *puts*. These have a bit of history behind them as well, but it's not quite worth getting into them for no good reason. After all, this is a book of theory, not one of context.

So going on, the term *call* essentially means the right to buy by a certain point of expiry, in American terms. This means that by the point at which the contract expires, you are able to exercise the options contract in the way that you see fit by buying at the term which is specified.

The term *put* means just the opposite. The term *put* refers to the idea of a right to *sell* at a certain price by a certain point of expiry, once more in American terms. This means that by the point that the contract expires, you can exercise the options contract in order to *sell* at the term which is specified.

There are essentially two parts to the whole *options contracts* equation: the holder and the writer. The holder is the person who *holds* the contract, and the *writer* is the person who writes the contract and is offering the given put or call to the other.

I'll go into finer detail on exactly the ways that these concepts can be more in depth momentarily. But first, we need to establish when options are actually useful.

Speculation

The first case in which you'd want to use them of *speculation*. Speculation is generally thought of as the simple notion of riding the tide of the market, essentially gambling on whether a security is going to gain value. However, there's one good point to options that raises it above other forms of securities such as stocks and bonds in terms of speculation. This is because since options are so versatile - one can, with options, assume that the market will either go up or down or even completely tank, and then bet according to that. With other securities, the manner in which you're able to speculate is limited *solely* to upward trends.

However, this can be just as negative as it can be positive. In fact, the odds are heavily pushed against anybody working with options, especially commoners. This is for the simple reason that working with options for speculation means that you're not only assuming that a stock or commodity will either grow in price or shrink in price, but also that you know the time frame within which this will happen.

However, much like gambling at a casino or anywhere else, options will have very high payouts should you be right in your prediction. This is one of the most common uses for options, in fact, but it's also one of the riskiest around, for various different reasons. Here, I'll try to extrapolate: if you are an amateur trader, you know nothing. That is the frankest and purest I can be about that. As somebody who is just playing the industry from the outside, you know absolutely nothing.

There's a bit of power in this knowledge, but there's also a lot of risk. There's one big factor which separates you from other people out there who are also trading options: the vast majority of people involved in options trading are parts of absolutely massive options trading firms. What this means, essentially, is that they are part of a business which specializes in analyzing stocks and commodities and then making the absolute best decisions that they can based off of the knowledge that they have at that point. However, the fact that they're likely wealthy and part of a major firm that operates in trading sets up a big distinction between you and them: they often are well connected. What does this mean for their business? Well, what it basically means is that they are very well off and have quite a bit of insider knowledge that lets them know how something is going to go beforehand.

Think back to our example from Thales of Ancient Greece: why did he take the actions that he did? The reason was largely that he had reason to believe that the olive harvest would be bigger than usual to a certain degree, so he acted on it.

Now imagine a bunch of major commodity industries which intertwine and work off of one another in this way or that and all meet in the middle at these options firms where expert financial analysts will make sense of the information from the absolutely numerous industries that they have to work off of. The end result is that you have little to no power or knowledge of where things are headed compared to them, which means that by default they are more likely to make more informed decisions concerning options trading than you are.

What else does this mean? Well, it essentially means that by simply trying to trade options as an amateur, you are in the bottom fifty percent of people who trade options at all. Your chances of success are not high and the odds are overwhelmingly stacked against you.

Does this mean you shouldn't work with options trading? No, not at all. It just means that as a beginning options trader, the odds are most certainly not in your favor.

Anyhow, that's the very basics of speculation and its usage with options trading. The next major usage of options trading finds its home in the concept of hedging. What exactly is this?

Hedging

Hedging is essentially a way to make certain that your investments won't totally turn sour. It's not terribly cost-efficient, but it does serve as a form of insurance against your investments going bad.

Many people will actually criticize this manner of profit protection. The philosophy is such that if you're so uncertain about the stocks and commodities in which you're investing, you shouldn't be investing in them at all - such is a poor financial decision that shouldn't really be made in the first place.

That's not to say that there isn't credence to that line of thought, but saying such is ignoring how incredibly useful hedging strategies can be. Hedging strategies can be used in order to save a lot of money that would otherwise be lost due to a poor investment. So how does this work?

Let's say that you wanted to make a large investment into a tech company such as Netflix. You were prepared to invest several thousand into Netflix. This by itself isn't too risky of a financial decision, as Netflix is a well off company that seems to only be trending upward -- provided you had the capital to make such a decision worthwhile. However, what if the CEO of Netflix were to get caught up in a sex trafficking ring, and the stock prices plummeted? All of a sudden, the n thousand that you invested into Netflix is now worth a fraction of what it was worth. An options contract would have prevented you from losing so much money.

This is because when you signed up for the options contract on your stocks, you would have made an agreement allowing you to sell your shares at a certain price. So if you had an options contract to sell your shares at the same rate which you bought them, and the real price of the shares dropped by even 300%, barring some stipulation in the contract (a "minimum" and "maximum" drop rate, so to speak), you would have been allowed to sell the stocks at the rate which you bought them - keeping you from losing any money.

We'll go more into hedging, but this is the basic idea behind it and why it's a good idea t certain times. Of course the situation which I described is an oddball which has little basis in reality, but more bizarre things have happened in the world of finance. Granted, drastic changes are rare enough that trying to set up an options contract for every investment you make would most certainly be overkill. However, if you're making heavy investments, it's definitely a bright idea to set up some sort of protection for yourself that way you aren't completely in the dark and suffering gigantic losses should things go south after all.

Hedging is primarily used by major financial institutions that are investing a lot of money into certain ventures because it offers enough insurance in the investment that if something *should* go wrong, they'll have enough after losing very little relatively at the end of the contract.

Employee Stock Options

The last major way in which you'll see options manifest is the usage of employee stock options. You've probably heard of these at one point or another. These are highly used among executives or for exceptionally talented employees, especially in order to attract very high caliber talent to the table (or keep them there when they already working for the company in question. Management at any level, especially very skilled management, will also often be given similar stock option positions. These are just ordinary options in many ways in that they exist in order to establish a certain relationship between a buyer and seller. Indeed, these employee options function very similarly to normal stock options because they allow the holder of the option the *ability* - though not at all the obligation - to buy company stock at a certain price. They differ in that where normal stock options are generally transactions between two entities who are unrelated in any way to the company whose stock is being acted upon, the employee stock options offer a different frame of reference in that they operate as a link between an *employer* and an *employee* rather than between two unrelated entities. Regardless of the connection, stock options offer the holding employee a very specific opportunity: to buy the company's stock at a certain rate within a certain time frame. This can be a fantastic opportunity depending upon where you're working and the rate at which they're allowing you to buy stock. Indeed, it can be the fastest way to build equity in a company, and given the choice between an employee stock option and a bonus, you generally should always take the stock option (if you've got the money to invest.)

As I've said before, we'll go more into the details of these exact practices and their uses momentarily, but for right now, I think it's of the utmost importance that we cover the most basic aspects of how a normal options trading scenario works out in a technical sense.

Chapter 3: In Practice - How does Option Trading Work?

In this chapter, we're going to be doing a basic shakedown of options and how they play out in a real life investment scenario. So in this example, we're going to say that there's a major craze in America, and tea shops are now the next big thing. There's a monolith in the industry that's absolutely taking over the markets called Gentle Leaf Tea Company. Gentle Leaf is growing in absolutely substantial numbers, and you think it's a bright idea to invest in the cost of their stock. How would you go about doing this, and would it be a bright idea after all?

For this scenario, let's say that it's the first of March, and the stock price of Gentle Left Tea Company is around $50 for each share. To go further, we have to talk about *strike prices*.

"Strike price" generally refers to the price at which a contract may be put into action in the context of market transactions. These contracts are generally stock options but can also be index options. Essentially, the strike price of a call option is the price at which a security is able to be bought until the expiration date; the strike price of a put option is the price at which a security is able to be sold until the expiration date.

Because this is the price at which a given contract is able to be exercised, strike prices are also referred to as *exercise prices* rather often.

Strike prices are essentially, in other words, the n value in an options contract which allows the holder to buy or sell a stock at a given price regardless of the market's weather. Generally, strike prices are written in 2.5 set or 5 set increments, so like "$60, $65, $70, ..." and so forth.

We can find the profitability of a bare transaction - a transaction of *strike price* and *market price*, or the price of the product without the options - by figuring out the difference between the strike price and the market price. There is a lot more which goes into this, of course; options have a certain premium, and this also doesn't even take into account the notion of commissions to the options broker that you'll have to pay.

But it's not at all a realistic example if we don't take those into account, so we're going to make up at the very least a fake option premium for this example. The commission could be any number of crazy off the wall values, so we're going to leave that out for right now, but it's important to take note of that in actual scenarios where you find yourself buying or trading options. Commissions will most certainly play a certain factor in your trade and may very well make the difference between some profit and none at all.

Anyhow, a stock option contract generally represents the opportunity for the holder to buy or sell 100 shares at a certain price. So, let's do some math in order to figure out an approximate value of a given transaction. Let's head back to the example of Gentle Leaf Tea Company. If our stock value is 50 for a share, then we're saying we want to buy at least 100 shares. Let's say that the strike price is about $55. Let's also say that we wanted to have the expiration date be in May so we have a good two months to feel this stock out and see where it goes. Let's assume that our stock premium per share is $2.75.

Perfect. So starting out on day one, we can chart out some pertinent values, like so:

- The *stock* price is at *fifty dollars per share*.
- The *option* price right now is just the premium per share, so $2.75.
- Right now, the *contract* - without any gain or loss accounted for - is $315.

Perfect. Now let's say we fast forward about 3 weeks to the twenty-first of March. On March 21st, let's assume that the price of the stock rose about ten dollars to a grand total of $60.

Since our strike price was $55, we're technically $5 "in the money", meaning over the strike value. This gives us our stock price, but it also lets us figure something else out: our *option* price. The *option* price is the price of the premium per share, in addition to how much we are "in the money".

So in this example, we are five dollars in the money and we had a $2.75 premium. This would allow us to calculate that the *option* price at this point would be about $7.75.

However, there's more to take into account! The general price of an option contract after a certain factor of time can most often be calculated by taking into account its *intrinsic value* and its *time value*. The intrinsic value can be remembered as the general amount that a person is *in the money* - so if a contract's strike price is $45, and the stock is at $55, then the person holding the contract is $10 in the money and the intrinsic value of the option premium is thusly $10. Time value takes into account the potential of an option to increase in value in the time it has left prior to expiry. Generally, in order to find the premium of an option, you would add these two together in order to find the worth.

However, a great number more variables can go into option pricing. For example, the projected volatility of an aspect can impact how much a premium might cost initially. "Volatility" in this sense refers to the propensity up to a given point of a stock to have relatively high amounts of fluctuation. That is to say that a stock which is more stable is less likely to have a significantly higher premium solely because of its volatility, as it has proven itself over time to not be terribly volatile. Meanwhile, a stock which has a tendency to fluctuate will be deemed more volatile and have a higher price generally.

Another thing which might well have an impact on the price of an option contract is *interest rates*, which often go unaccounted for because they have somewhat small effects compared to others. However, their effects certainly aren't negligible and it's certainly worth your time to learn how they can affect the pricing of your premiums. *Interest rates* have the following effect, and it's rather simple to follow: if the interest rates increase, then the premiums for *buying* as the holder will rise, while the premiums for *selling* as the holder will fall. Conversely, if the interest rates are to decrease, the premiums for *selling* as the holder will rise, while the premiums for *buying* as the holder will fall. This is due to the fact that the price of owning the stock itself will rise exponentially as the interest rates rise, and thus the buyer on either side of the deal will end up having to pay far higher interest rates in the end.

The last thing which can really have an impact on the price of option contracts is *dividends*. Dividends are able to impact options prices due to the fact that the price of the stock itself will drop by the amount of cash dividend as accords to the ex-dividends. Dividends will result in the following price modulations: if the dividend on the stock itself should rise, the premiums for a *buying holder* will decrease and the premiums for a *selling holder* will increase; if the dividend on the stock itself should fall, then the premiums for a *buying holder* will increase, and the premiums for a *selling holder* will decrease.

Anyhow, there are a lot of things which will ultimately affect the price of an option premium, but the key things which affect it most are the *intrinsic value* and the *time value*. Anyhow, let's go back to our example of the Gentle Leaf Tea Company: to this point, we've calculated that we had a $2.75 premium per share and we were $5 in the money, meaning that the market price of the stock was $5 over the strike price on the options contract. However, we also have to account for *time value*. There are a lot of factors which inherently influence this specifically, like a stock's volatility, but the idea is that the longer a stock has until expiry, the greater the chance that at some point between point n in time and the expiration date, the stock will be over the strike price and therefore profitable. Let's assume a 30 cents per share time value, which means that we have $2.75 (the premium per share) + $5 (amount over the strike price) + $.30 (the time value of the stock). So, a single share is worth $8.05 at this point. So how much of a profit have we made?

You can find the profit that you've made by subtracting your *initial* contract price and subtracting it (here being $2.75) from your *current* contract price (here being $8.05) and multiplying that by 100 (one for each share, with 100 shares total.)

Doing this math would give us something like:
8.05 - 2.75 = 5.30
5.30 * 100 = 530

So off of our option alone (and a really successful prediction, but I digress), we've made roughly $530 dollars in profit. That's a lot to make off of a simple options trade. Bear in mind that you'd also have to pay commission on this, but that's a given.

Now let's say, for example, that you didn't want to sell on March 21st, and instead you wanted to ride it out and see if the stock goes higher. So, you sit on the stock for quite a while, but it starts to go down and continues to tank up until your expiry date. On the expiry date, you've made a net loss of $275 dollars, the total cost of your contract. Your option is entirely worthless because it's the expiration date.

Additionally, if your option is below the strike price, you can't enact the option just by the nature of the agreement. Your option is essentially worthless.

The important thing to remember in basic options trading is that your money is not glued down in any way. That is to say that you aren't obligated to make a purchase or a sale when you're the holder of the contract. I know I've said this a few times, but now seems a better time than any to really expound upon it.

There are two sides to an options contract: the *holder* and the *writer*. The *writer* is the person who draws up the options contract and offers it to the other person. The writer could be the person either buying or selling the commodity or stock in question. The distinction is rather silly. The *holder* is the person who is actively holding the options track and is able to exercise it if they wish.

The holder is *not* obligated to buy or sell according to

their options contract, but the writer is obligated to buy or sell on their end if the option contract is carried through. This means that if the writer is selling, they have to set aside stock and carry through, legally, if the person on the other end decides that they would like to carry through on the options contract. If the writer is buying something from the seller, they *have* to have the capital to invest in the options contract should the holder choose to sell.

Chapter 4: Where to Trade Options

There's a lot of contention about what is the best place to trade options. Really, it depends upon your individual needs. Note that a lot of over-the-counter options trading still happens today and likely makes up the bulk of "options" contracts-style transactions. However, it's still worthwhile, should you decide that you truly want to invest in options, to know what sites are the best and for what reasons.

First, there are generally two sites which are seen as the "best" for options trading: optionsXpress and TradeStation. Both of these have their own perks and their own reasons that you may decide to work through them.

OptionsXpress is a great place to start because they don't have an account minimum. They do ask a $12.95 commission on trades, and OptionsXpress only takes $1.25 for each contract. The fees can be a tad iffy depending upon your trade volume but generally, the fees are low compared to other options. The other great thing about options trading by way of optionsXpress is that they have a lot of features that you'd really come expecting. For example, they offer real time quotes, and also allow you to look at options chains. Even better, optionsXpress doesn't charge you extra at all for using these tools. Bear in mind that in the world of finance, platforms will *always* favor those who are able to move more shares and who trade more often. But with that said, as far as a cost effective options trading platform, OptionsXpress has you covered.

If you have a bit of money to invest, then you can go with *TradeStation*. TradeStation is generally ranked up there with optionsXpress in terms of really strong options trading platforms. And indeed, it's hard to find one much better than TradeStation. In exchange for a bit of a hefty account minimum, TradeStation offers you a huge amount of useful tools tucked right into their super handy platform. For example, you'll find yourself using features like automatic trade execution rather often. TradeStation is also built for people who understand technology such that they can develop, test, and sell their own trading strategies to other enterprising investors who may have an interest in such a thing. Of course, this doesn't mean necessarily that you *have* to use this utility, but it can certainly help you should you decide to use it. It has a high price tag with it, but it's very difficult to find a platform that is much better than TradeStation at what it's supposed to do: be a simple and straightforward platform which is highly extensible and super easy to build upon, should that be what you're wanting.

However, these can get rather convoluted. What if you just wanted simple, low-cost, and easy to understand, then it's hard to beat *eOption.* eOption is fantastic for low-capital investors who want the platform to just simply get out of their way and let them do their own thing. eOptions has an account minimum of $500, which isn't too much in terms of options trading, and their rates are extremely flat. They take a $3 trade commission, as well as fifteen cents for every contract that you decide to be involved with. If you haven't traded two times in the last year, or if you have less than ten thousand dollars in either your credit balances or your debit balances, you'll pay a fifty dollar fee for "account inactivity". They have an incredibly low margin rate, which means that their trading costs are low. The only place that you might get caught up is that they have a lot of data fees and platform fees. These can be a veritable cash rainbow of prices, and clock in at anywhere from $1 to $200 in a month, or possibly even more depending upon what all you're doing on the platform. As far as design and ease of use, there's not too much that's different from the others; there are an array of features that are available to you. Nothing particularly stand-out or amazing, but it certainly isn't a drab platform either. It's well-featured and if you just want a simple and low-cost platform other than optionsXpress, it's incredibly difficult to find something that will fill those shoes better than eOptions.

In terms of powerful trading platforms, there are two reigning kings: TD Ameritrade and OptionsHouse. Both have their own perks. Either one of these has one of the most high tech and fully loaded trading platforms that you can ask for, as well as with specifically useful features that you as the end user will find especially neat and handy.

TD Ameritrade doesn't have an account minimum and it takes a $9.99 trade commission. In addition, they have a promotion running which gives you six hundred dollars when you make a certain deposit. That can certainly be alluring in its own and give you a bit of extra capital to work with. TD Ameritrade operates on one of the most revered trading platforms in the business. Known as *thinkorswim*, this platform is specifically created for active investors who are wanting the opportunity to get their hands on high quality tools and research, as well as who would like to try out different strategies or practice cost observation by analyzing the risks and benefits of certain interactions they could make on the marketplace. In addition, TD Ameritrade offers the *Trade Architect* service, based on the internet, as well as a Mobile Trader application for smartphones and other mobile devices. Should one use *Trade Architect* instead of *thinkorswim*, they'll find it lacking a bit in tools and services compared to the awe-inspiring *thinkorswim*, but nevertheless they'll still find an absolute wealth of complex features that they'll find useful regardless.

The other super impressive platform that one may be interested in is aligned with the *OptionsHouse* eTrade broker. They offer a huge array of tools which are usually relegated to financial professionals who make an absolute career out of carefully watching and analyzing the markets in different ways. In other words, they have a huge number of tools that will benefit the type who wants to be an active trader. OptionsHouse too has a decent trade commission: $4.95 per trade. They don't have a specific account minimum, and they offer a thousand dollars in free commissions when you make a certain deposit.

Lastly, there are a couple platforms which offer a great amount of utility in another way: the absolute wealth of market research and market data that they'll have available for free to any enterprising users who decide to use these services. In this category are *Charles Schwab* and *Fidelity.*

Fidelity has a $7.95 trade commission and a $2,500 account minimum. However, in return for this hefty minimum and hefty commission rate, you get access to one of the best stores of knowledge in the industry. They get a huge amount of research, bigger than almost anybody else, and they offer a lot of research from over twenty industry giants, such as McLean Capital Management. They make it super easy to access all of this and it also comes free with your account. They also offer an application for your mobile device which lets you access all of the research by way of your phone's built-in web browser. If you're looking for raw research, it's hard to do any better than using Fidelity Investments as your broker.

However, there is a tad more to knowledge than simply research, and *Charles Schwab* excels where Fidelity falls short.

They have a $6.95 trade commission and a $1,000 account minimum. Additionally, they'll give you five hundred dollars in cash if you make a certain deposit, which once again could be useful for building up some expendable capital to use for your trading. In addition to a lot of raw research, Schwab has a tremendous amount of support for active traders, offering things such as trade assessment tools to allow you to see whether or not a trade you'd like to make is a bright idea. However, they also offer to you a ton of options market discourse by the analysts hired by Schwab, as well as seminars, both live and pre-recorded, both online and in-person. What's more is that the in person seminars are free to users of the service, because Schwab has a lot of branches throughout the country. What's more is that Schwab offers two top-notch platforms for stock trading. One is geared towards newer options traders, called *StreetSmart*, and the other is geared towards far more active traders, called StreetSmart Edge.

Really, knowing what options broker to go with is a matter of knowing yourself and your situation. Do you have a lot to spend on options trading? If you don't have a lot of investment capital, it's much better to start small and not invest too much in the first place, since your capital matters more to you by virtue of there being less of it. If you have a lot of investment capital and a basic idea of how to trade options, you'd be served well to go with one of the more research-heavy brokers geared at active traders. That too is a consideration in and of itself; do you want trading to be a significant part of your life? For example, do you want to do more with trading than just check the market every morning before work and night before bed? Do you want to spend a significant amount of time working on your portfolio and evaluating specific decisions to see which one would result in you making the biggest profit? If so, then you might find that you'd find yourself happier in the ones with a greater wealth of tools.

Chapter 5: Avoiding Common Mistakes

Options are very risky, full stop. There are a lot of places where things can go wrong, and what's more is that it's extremely easy for people newer to the industry to make really simple mistakes that only take a little knowledge and foresight to avoid. The point of this chapter is to analyze these mistakes that a huge number of beginners will make so that you can avoid making them yourself and, hopefully, be a better investor yourself.

MISTAKE #1: BUYING CHEAP CALL OPTIONS

Buying calls is absolutely not bad in and of itself. But buying cheap calls can be very dangerous, and this is for a multitude of reasons. But before we discuss why it's dangerous, we have to examine why people do this in the first place.

The main reason that people are duped into buying especially cheap call options that are way beyond any sort of reality is, first off, because they're cheap. The low-price tag may present itself as a sort of "gambling" rather than "investment", but even if you're gambling, it's not much of a gamble if there's over an eighty percent likelihood that you'll end up losing the bet.

The other reason that one may be a cheap call option is because it fits a paradigm that they're accustomed to. After all, when you buy a call option, you're just making the prediction that the stock will go up in price, right? And that's the notion that a lot of people make when they're selling *equities*. The whole "buy low, sell high" paradigm absolutely rules the sphere of equity trading. So this is a comfortable paradigm to transfer over to options trading. It doesn't feel too far off from what you know.

However, this is a terrible idea to transfer over, and I'll tell you why: when you buy cheap options, you are buying options which are cheap for a very specific reason. Remember how we talked about things that can affect options premiums? Well, that lesson should apply here. Low cost options contracts are low cost because they aren't expected to pay out well; they're low demand, so the broker doesn't have to ask much in order to make a decent amount off of it.

What's more is that when you buy options on a stock, as we've already discussed, you're already taking into account the timing of a stock hitting a high or a low. Its price will be affected by the likelihood of it going in a specific direction.

In other words, cheap call options are generally cheap because they aren't going to go anywhere, and you'd have to have a miracle and a half to not lose the entirety of your options premium that you paid down, let alone make a profit.

So what can you as a beginner do instead? You should build your equities portfolio and instead *write* calls on stocks that *you own*, rather than *holding* calls on stocks that *others* own. When you do so, what you're basically saying is that you'll sell the stock that you own at the strike price in the option. Since in calls, the price is generally higher than the *strike price*, the risk is minimal. You, as the writer, are simply saying to the holder "if the stock goes up to the strike price, I will sell it at that price, even if it is above the strike price." This means that regardless of what happens, you make a profit, it's just not *quite* as high as it would be otherwise.

This technique is called the "covered call". It's a great way to make a fair amount of early income, and it's relatively safe for you as the writer. The only way that this method could displace your capital is if the stock goes significantly down (more than normal market fluctuations) since the time that you'd invested in it. However, it does limit your ability to sell if your stock goes exponentially up, as it gives you an "earnings" ceiling. But regardless - though you may not become a multimillionaire off of one stock boom, you'll make a steady profit off of selling contracts to your investments.

Moreover, if the market doesn't really go anywhere and just stays flat, and your stock's market price never hits the strike price, you still obtain the premium from the contract buyer for selling him the option in the first place. Meanwhile, you maintain your stock, of course, to repeat the process once more once the expiry date has been reached on a given contract.

So this is a much safer way to get to know the options market as you're just starting out and make a steady amount of income rather than simply going gung-ho on certain out of the money calls. What's more is that instead of putting you in a position to take *risks*, you're putting yourself in a position to be the *risk which others take*. You are in a secure position; if the market stays flat, or goes down a bit, you collect a small premium and maintain your stock. If the market rises to the stock price, you still profit - though maybe not as much as you would have liked to - and can use the resultant capital in order to invest in another stock and repeat the process. The only risk you're undertaking in this scenario is the possibility that your invested capital is devalued. However, the chances of a major crash are much lower, and you still have a certain amount of steady income from the covered calls on the stock.

MISTAKE #2: NO PLAN

This is a critical killer. With anything, it's important to have a "way out" if things don't go your way, and be able to control your emotional reactions should things shift for the worse. However, it's of absolutely paramount importance in the trading game, in a manner which really can't be understated at all. Having a plan is important in every single trade that you'll ever make, and having a sort of "exit" plan is most definitely important, too.

So what do I mean by "have a plan"? It's simple. You need to have a plan in place that you can minimize losses if your trades go for the worse and maximize gains if they go for the better. And this doesn't necessarily mean forming some sort of bizarre clairvoyance for the market and knowing exactly what's going to happen.

Rather, it's about recognizing patterns and developing a finite way for yourself to react to these patterns. This is absolutely imperative, actually. If you don't do this, then you're going to find yourself taking massive losses waiting for an option to go in the money as you near your expiry date, or you're going to find your options taking turns for the worse because you wanted to wait around and see if a stock would continue to go up.

You need to set up a plan for yourself: what sort of gains will make you happy as a trader when you're on the upside? What is the worst you'll allow things to get on the downside before dodging out? Evaluate how trades have gone wrong before and specifically factor in for those. Do you have a habit of getting a bit greedy and losing good deals because a given stock did a 180 and ended up losing more than you would have gotten otherwise? Do you have a habit of holding onto stocks for too long when they're bad and losing more money than is necessary in the process? Identify those and specifically set up plans for those traits in particular.

MISTAKE #3: ILLIQUIDITY

Liquidity essentially means the ease with which a person can buy or sell something without there being a significant change in the price of that thing. This means that there must always be a large amount of active traders within the market. In a mathematical sense, liquidity as a concept represents the likelihood that the following trade will be around the same price as the prior one, preferably with the two trades being of equal price.

Options markets are by their nature less liquid than stock markets are because stock markets operate on a simple notion of equity. You sell a share, you buy a share, that share represents the essential concept of a piece of something bigger, but there's little way to change that share. That share is that share, basically. Options markets, however, offer a variety of different contracts. On an options markets, one may buy a long call option, a long put option, a short call option, a short put option, and any variation of options contracts therein. They can buy American style options or British style options. They generally have a lot more variance in both the mechanisms of trade as well as the things which are being traded themselves. Because of this, options markets *are* far less liquid than stock markets, because there's so much more variance for people to account for.

A company which trades constantly is unlikely to be a liquidity issue, regardless of whether you're operating on the stock market or the options market. However, if a company is smaller or has stock which trades far less frequently, then it's much more illiquid.

It follows that if a given stock should be illiquid, because of the different mechanisms at work then the options contracts available to that same company will be even more illiquid. This means that the bid and ask price for options become very artificially distant. This means that a lot of money would be spent in order just to establish a position. (stock lingo for "buy it"; "clear your position" means to sell stock)

So what can you do to prevent this? The easiest way is to avoid trading illiquid options, simply put. Research every single investment you make very well, and be certain that the interest in the stock is incredibly high. Trading illiquid assets can be a massive setback and cost you far more than you'd make off of it, and it will save you a lot of stress too. There are a huge number of opportunities for good liquid options contracts that are readily available to you.

Trading options can be incredibly difficult. Here, I only put the three most egregious examples which came to mind, but all of them are extremely common and admittedly tempting mistakes that beginner traders will make in the world of options trading. It's important that if you want to grow as a trader, you recognize as many of *other* people's mistakes as you can. If you do so, you're making silently sure that you don't make those same mistakes yourself, in effect making you a far better trader than you would be otherwise.

So the takeaway of this chapter is this: learn from others, not just their successes but their mistakes too. If you do so, you'll be on the path to being an expert financial analyst and trader.

Chapter 6: Research before Trading

Before you do anything else, it's of the utmost importance that you spend a fair amount of time getting to learn the basics of everything that you're working with. There are any variety of ways that you might have ended up here. You may be a finance student or you may just be somebody wanting to make strong market decisions and start investing. Regardless, my job throughout this book is to leave you feeling at the end of it like you know a lot more than you did at the start of it.

There's a lot of terminology and theory behind options trading, and frankly, it's impossible to cover every single thing in this book. And what's more is that I wouldn't want to; I have the humility to admit that I'm not the best trader. Nobody's the best trader, though. Everybody has their own methods of trading and their own strategies that they've developed over time to help them become absolute behemoths on the market and expert traders in their own right.

Because of this, it's better that you learn from *everyone* that you can. What does this mean? Well, there are a wealth of options trading resources out there. You should absolutely explore them.

However, in exploring them, you'll find that a lot of them aren't that great, or are just repeating the same thing. It's pretty difficult to find a worthwhile options resource because options are a hot button issue that a lot of people are interested in right now. Merely writing about options means that you're guaranteed to get some page views, and a lot of people exploit this and generate less than great content without ever even really having a lot of exposure to trading.

To help you to recognize good options sites, I've compiled a list of several so that you could learn more of what to look for and what makes a strong options resource.

We'll start with the **CBOE**, which is just the go-to for every single serious options trader. This is one of, if not the, largest resources for options in general, and has a huge amount of information regarding both the volume and the activity of given options. Specifically, you should check out their community at http://communities.cboe.com/. Why is this? Because a ton of leaders from the options trading industry gather here in order to talk about everything that's happening on the market, share strategies, and discuss how to become a better investor.

Another extremely important one that you'd be silly to ignore is Dan Sheridan's **Sheridan Mentoring**, at http://www.sheridanmentoring.com/. Dan Sheridan is a very able options trader with a lot of skill and knowledge, but perhaps more importantly, he's a very exceptional teacher. Because of this, he's a great resource to go to for any options trader, whether they're a beginner or a veteran, because he always has ways to help people advance in ways they likely hadn't even thought possible.

Also impossible to ignore is **The Options Insider** at http://www.theoptionsinsider.com/. What's so great about The Options Insider? Well, despite the fact that the site is relatively young, it's still jam-packed with a whole lot of extremely useful information that you'll find endlessly handy. For example, there are industry insights, a lot of reviews on upcoming products, interviews with pertinent leaders in the options industry, and a whole lot of options market commentary to boot. So when you head to The Options Insider, you'll find yourself absolutely awash in relevant information that will be extremely easy for you to ascertain, but you're not really going to ever hit a point where this site also can't teach you something new and handy. In short, this site is a great one for learning precisely how to become a better options trader, and no smart investor would ignore such a great resource.

There's no shortage of amazing communities and resources for you to access as a new and budding options trader. You're going to find yourself actually with too many and having to weed through worse ones, but you will most certainly be able to find some that attend very well to your needs.

I figure that there's one last thing I really have to teach you before I bring this book to a close: how do you read a gosh-darn options table?

An options table has a ton of information on it, and it can be a little difficult to parse. Here's the easiest way to parse it.

The first column will most generally be the important ones in determining options regarding the specifics on the option itself. Take the following:

IBM MAY17 120 C

What does this mean? It means that its an option for the stock with the ticker symbol *IBM*, the month and year of expiration (*MAY17* meaning *May of 2017*), the strike price (120 means the stock must reach 120 for the contract to be valid), and whether a contract is a call or a put (*C* meaning, of course, *call*).

There will also generally be "bid" and "ask" columns. In options trading, *bid* means the last price to be offered by a trader to buy a given option. *Ask* means, just the opposite, and refers to the last price offered by a trader to sell a given option.

There also are a lot of other metrics. Some are less important than others, but all correspond to the health of a particular option in various scenarios.

The *volume* column tells you how many options contracts of a specific sort were traded over the course of the last trading session. *Open interest* will indicate the total contracts of a given option that have been created, written, and set up but have yet to be met.

The *strike* column is, of course, the strike price of the option. This is generally listed in the first column as well, but it does have its own column as well.

Options tables are immensely sophisticated and there's a huge amount of information that is managed to be represented in a very small surface area. However, all of this information can have a result upon your outcome and should be taken very seriously. As a beginner, you can mostly get away with knowing the basics (bid, ask, symbols, strike prices, and so on) but if you want to be an active trader, you certainly need to devote time to learning about things such as delta bid/asks and gamma bid/asks and so forth.

Conclusion

Thank for making it through to the end of *Options Trading: A Quick and Easy Guide for Beginners to Start Trading*, let's hope it was informative and able to provide you with all of the tools you need to achieve your goals whatever it may be.

The next step is to implement all of this. Learn, learn, learn, and at some point take the jump to invest and start learning by experience.

I feel like I need to reiterate this one last time for good measure: options trading is dangerous. It's not something that you can just passively be involved in, and honestly, it's not a good place for any beginning trader to get involved in. It takes a lot of extensive theory and knowledge about exactly the things you're working with, and you're going to find often that you'll be losing instead of gaining -- especially as a beginner trader.

What are the ways to circumvent this? Well, there isn't. The obvious route is to simply go with something more lucrative and less risky. For example, if you just invest in equities and indexes, you can expect something like a six percent growth rate. After all, the economy is growing constantly. Neoliberal economic policies only exacerbate this sense of growth such that if you can actually afford to make a reasonable investment into equities or indexes, you will almost certainly see a positive return on it, albeit a smaller one.

Some time ago, before I devoted myself to studying finances and learning how to be a good investor, driven mainly by an intense interest in the way that the markets ticked and worked and the way that wealth moved around in our economy, a friend shared with me some very pertinent advice: "you're better off investing in yourself than investing in stocks." Since then, that's somewhat resonated.

Investments are called investments for a reason: they're long-term investments intended to accrue a certain amount of revenue over time, and if the company in which you invested does well, you too will benefit from the resultant success of course. That's the nature of investments.

But it's also a very impersonal and unsure way to make money. If you're looking for a get rich quick scheme, this is not it. Investing has a whole lot of upsides and can be a lot of fun and an absolutely crazy ride. But that doesn't mean that it's intended to make you a ton of money. If you're looking for localized investment with high returns, there are better ways to do it, such as learning about making money by affiliate marketing or creating worthwhile content.

The long and short of it is that investing is intended for people who have extra money. It's not intended for people to make extra money. Some just happen to. Most, in fact, do, but it's very, very unlikely that you're going to be the next Warren Buffet because of investment, especially in options trading.

And that goes further to say that if this is really what you want to do, be prepared to lose some money in the process. Options trading is hard to get into as a beginner, and take a fair amount of capital to even get a decent start. However, if you decide that it's what you want to do, here's how I can sum up the path for you going forward.

The first thing is to only even consider doing options trading with your speculative capital. What speculative capital means is money that you can set aside and essentially afford to lose should things go awry. Never, ever invest money that you genuinely need. Before doing any sort of investiture, be certain that you have at least 3 months of emergency savings set up and that you can afford to lose every single cent that you're putting into it. There's not a successful trader that won't tell you this. This isn't to turn you away from investing; it's a very real way to make very real capital gains... if you know what you're doing. But every single worthwhile trader out there will tell you to prepare to lose. Don't ever do anything that puts you in a worse position than you started out in. Only ever invest capital that you do not need.

The second thing is to spend a fair amount of time doing research. Research is ultimately the name of the game in any sort of investing. A part of me feels like that goes without saying, but it should be driven home that it is absolutely the case. Research is the fundamental crux of every decision that happens in the marketplace. It's only by knowing about a company, about its founder and its board and about its upcoming products, by knowing its past history and its marketplace trends, by knowing the trends of the market in general, by knowing what things like beta bid/ask are and how they have an impact on the viability of an options trade, and by knowing in-depth a lot of key concepts on the marketplace that you can even think of becoming a renowned options trader.

The third thing is far less general - you're going to have a much easier time starting out as an options trader if you build a portfolio and then proceed to sell contracts on those options. It will give you a much kinder sandbox with a lot less shards of glass where you can learn the ins and outs of options trading while still being a safe distance away from any real economic harm. Every single new options trader should spend a lot of time doing covered calls until they feel as though they sufficiently know the market and what they're doing and how they have a hand in the market at large.

In the end, if you feel like trading, you absolutely should. I genuinely hope that I've given you enough foundational information such that you can make informed decisions about the things you'll be doing on the market. Options trading, as I said, can be very lucrative if you know what you're doing. My goal in writing this book was to help set you up to know what you're doing.

So if you've made it past all my warnings and second-guesses and you've decided that you still definitely want to move forward on options trading, then what are you waiting for? Go back to one of the brokers we discussed in chapter four and start an account. Do some research before you make a deposit so that you're sure this is the step you want to take, and once you're positive, take the steps you have to to get into the game.

Options trading is endlessly fun and rewarding if you find yourself interested in these sort of things, and I can't help but feel like you'll very much enjoy your time spent doing it if you've made it this far into this book. So go for it!

Finally, if you found this book useful in anyway, a review on Amazon is always appreciated!